LET'S SIGN & DOWN SYNDROME

Signs for Children with Special Needs

CATH SMITH and Dr WENDY UTTLEY

Illustrated by Cath Smith

CO-SIGN COMMUNICATIONS

Incorporating Deafsign.com and DeafBooks.co.uk

ACKNOWLEDGEMENTS

My grateful thanks and appreciation for;

Help and advice at various times and at various stages on different projects that have helped to develop the bank of graphics that provide the basis of this publication, particularly for their work on the Level 1 sign vocabulary and materials to;

The Middlesbrough British Sign Language Tutor Group.

For help with converting and developing illustrations for the LET'S SIGN & WRITE BSL Graphics packs to;

Widgit Software Ltd.

With a special thank you for suggesting this publication and format, help with the new graphics, selection of sign vocabulary and expertise in Down syndrome to;

Dr Wendy Uttley of the Down Syndrome Support Group Bradford

First published 2008 Reprinted 2011, 2012, 2014

ISBN-10: 1-905913-02-8
ISBN-13: 978-1-905913-02-2

Published by Co-Sign Communications
Incorporating DeafBooks & DEAFSIGN
Stockton-on-Tees TS18 5HH
Tel: 01642 580505
email: cath@deafsign.com
email: info@deafbooks.co.uk
www.DeafBooks.co.uk

Distributed by Gardners Books

also available for retail and trade sales from
www.DeafBooks.co.uk

DeafBooks at Alphagraphics,
8-9 Vanguard Court, Preston Farm,
Stockton TS18 3TR

deafbooks@agnortheast.com

Telephone: 01642 525161
Fax: 01642 525121

Printed in Great Britain by AlphaGraphics North East

CONTENTS

FOREWORD

I'm pleased to have joined forces with Dr Wendy Uttley to produce this publication of British Sign Language (BSL) vocabulary to support the communication and spoken language development of children with Down syndrome, and for teachers and families who use signs to support children and adults with special needs.

BSL is the language of Britain's Deaf community to whom it is essential and highly valued. As a visual gestural language with its own grammar and spatial structures, it differs from spoken English - but in practice its vocabulary of signs is also used to support spoken language and is now believed beneficial to a wide range of learners because of its visual and kinaesthetic nature.

Using signs to support spoken language and communication with children and adults with special needs has gained widespread practice and acceptance, and the signs used are most usually from BSL vocabulary. Like spoken language, BSL does have regional 'dialects'. The signs used in this book are those that are commonly used and understood across the country and other versions are also available.

The LET'S SIGN BSL Series of dictionaries, posters, flashcards, and ebooks contain colourful, visually stimulating materials and include a graphic packs available on licence to make individualised, tailor-made items. Deaf and hearing professionals have worked together to develop this series to encourage and support sign language users of all ages and abilities and these materials are also proving popular with those who use other BSL based systems and materials.

We welcome requests for new work and collaboration with others to achieve this, as in this new publication. Dr Uttley's experience and expertise bring us a clear and accessible introduction to this field, with guidelines and suggestions for using signs with children, that will prove invaluable to parents and professionals. This book makes a welcome addition to the series, and can be used alongside our other materials to give help and support at different stages and in different ways.

The layout of this book provides a handy topic format, but please note that this is **not** a copyable resource, and is not priced as such. We believe that all children and their families have a right to good quality, interesting materials, and we strive to provide these at fair prices with discount available on multiple orders.

This book and all of our materials are subject to copyright law and cannot be copied without permission and we ask that this is please respected. However, for those who wish to make their own personalised materials, the **LET'S SIGN BSL** sign graphics are available to use on an annually renewable licence. A variety of licence options are available from www.DeafBooks.co.uk and more details are given on page 14.

All of our publications are printed and bound in this country, in our own locality. We are also developing paperless resources such as iphone and other mobile applications, ebooks, and low-price or free downloads that make ideal tasters and samples that can be printed or viewed on screen or whiteboard. See **www.DeafBooks.co.uk**

Cath Smith

INTRODUCTION

My son, Sam, now nine years old, has Down syndrome. We started signing with Sam in his first year to help develop his communication and language skills.

Over the years I have gained much expertise from working with children who have Down syndrome, their families and the professionals involved.

In my role as Group Coordinator and Trainer for the Down Syndrome Support Group Bradford, I now deliver training for both parents and professionals in the specific learning needs of children with Down syndrome. As a group we felt it was time to produce a publication outlining why and how to use signing and the benefits it can bring for all involved.

A VISUAL TOOL

When we use signs with children with Down syndrome we are using them as a bridge to talking. The emphasis must always be on the spoken word. Always remember to SAY the word when you sign it and always repeat the correct sign and spoken word when your child has attempted to sign/say a word.

Signing is used as a visual tool to reinforce the spoken word; it is easy to do and literally at your finger tips. At first you may feel a little self conscious, I know I did, but once you see the benefits it brings to the child, you will become more confident and relaxed in your signing. Encourage family, friends and school, both pupils and staff, to get involved and you'll soon see how much fun it is.

Once your child can sign, for example *DRINK PLEASE* do not give *them the drink just for signing but encourage them to speak as well, even if it is just an utterance. The spoken words 'drink please' can be encouraged by using the written words 'drink please' written on a flash card.

DIFFERENT SIGN SYSTEMS

When we sign with children who have Down syndrome, our aim is to support the use of speech, develop vocabulary, and to give confidence and encourage communication generally. We choose to use the vocabulary of BSL signs to do this, since BSL is widely used and recognised as a community language of this country.

BSL is the language of the Deaf community of Britain in which it flourishes as a full and complete language and is used independently of speech.

However in practice, there are various language and communication combinations to accommodate life in the hearing community. In the education of deaf children for example, there is a mixture of approaches. These include the use of BSL and English as separate languages (sign bilingualism) and other methods that effectively combine the two languages - using hearing aids, implants, speech and listening skills with the addition of BSL signs and this is known as Sign Supported English (SSE) or Total Communication.

* To avoid constant repetition of he/she, his/her, him/her we use the terms them, their and they.

Other speech supporting sign systems are also available such as Baby Signing for all pre-verbal youngsters, and Makaton and Signalong in the field of special needs. All of these systems are based on BSL and many of the signs are the same.

We have opted for the LET'S SIGN BSL graphics because of their clarity and appeal, in addition to the fact that they are part of a Series of dictionaries, posters and flashcards etc. that are ready to use at different stages. The sign graphics are also available in colour versions in Let's Sign & Write BSL graphics pack published by Widgit Software, for you to create your own personalised materials.

BSL is subject to regional variation in its vocabulary similar to accent and dialect in spoken language. We have tried to choose signs that are widely used and that are clear and simple to form and have worked together to develop and adapt these sign graphics to meet our specific needs. Included are a handful of created signs for function words that do not have signs in BSL, and this is made clear in their captions. The signs included in this book are the ones we have found to be most useful in working with a child who has Down syndrome.

In practice, most signing will be used in the early years, as the child's speech and vocabulary are developing (you can start signing from birth). As the child begins to speak and make themselves understood, they will begin to drop their signs; this is usually around the age of five or six. However we have found that signing can again become useful as the child progresses from from two/three word phrases, to fuller sentences. Signing, alongside the written word, helps to emphasise link words such as *THE* and *AND* and encourages longer sentences and interaction by using *WHY? BECAUSE, WHO? WHERE? WHAT?* etc.

GRAMMAR, SPELLING & CLARITY OF SPEECH

Signing and fingerspelling can also be used to help with grammar, spelling and pronunciation. For example;

- Grammar - you can make link words like *THE* and *AND* visual.
- Pronunciation - you can fingerspell key syllable letters in a long word or you can fingerspell initial letters to prompt correct pronunciation, eg. 'C' to emphasise *CARPET* rather than 'tarpet'.

THE WRITTEN WORD

Use of the written word is highly recommended to promote the development of grammar and pronunciation. It is another visual method and is very effective since the child can see the link words and word endings such as 'ed', 's', 'ing' and so on.

Moving onto the written word: When your child is signing, the emphasis must always be on speech. Later the written word is introduced as another visual tool to encourage speaking in sentences. For example, you would not sign the whole of 'I am reading a book'. If you wanted to encourage a child to practise saying all of these words you would use a sentence strip displaying these words.

DOWN SYNDROME: WHY USE SIGNING?

Children with Down syndrome are usually good visual learners - you will most probably have witnessed your child mimicking your gestures many times.

While you are talking you scratch your nose and what does your child do?
They scratch their own nose. Children with Down syndrome can easily copy gesture but not sounds.

Signing grabs a child's attention and focuses them on the speaker. The sign then gives visual 'speech' so the child sees the word as well as hears it.

From birth all children are immersed in sound and begin to store these sounds ready to produce speech.

Research shows that a child with Down syndrome has difficulty storing sounds, not just because they may have been hearing incorrectly (80% of children with Down syndrome have glue ear or some form of hearing loss) but also because their auditory memory does not function as well as a child without Down syndrome.

In a nutshell if it goes in through their eyes they have a better chance of recalling it later.

For example, my son Sam had been trying to say the word *vegetable* for months - a four syllable word - too long for Sam to store in his short term memory, but shown the sign only once he was, and still is, able to produce the sign for *vegetable* without prompt.

THE BENEFITS OF SIGNING

- Signing to a child attracts their attention, slows down your speech and makes your words visual. Making a word visual enables the child to hold the word in their head for longer and improves their concentration and understanding.

- Signing helps to reduce the amount you say.

- Encouraging a child to sign enables them to communicate more fully and helps you to understand what they are trying to say.

- Being able to sign reduces frustration for both adult and child. Children with Down syndrome often understand much more than they can say.

- Signs help support good communication and language teaching - we can introduce new vocabulary with the aid of signs.

- A child will switch to using a sign if their speech is not understood. For example, Sam no longer signs *MORE* but if he is asking a stranger for *more* and finds he is not being understood he will sign it.

THE ROLE OF THE WRITTEN WORD

It is suggested by Professor Sue Buckley OBE, of the Down Syndrome Educational Trust, Portsmouth, that the written word is also very useful as a visual support to learning new words, grammar and improving pronunciation.

For example, the sign for *VEGETABLE* will help Sam communicate the word *vegetable* but it will not help him to say it more clearly, other than he will hear the word as you say it in response to his signing. However the written word shows Sam the letters and visually helps his speech.

As mentioned earlier in the Introduction, we do not sign all of the words in a sentence. Once your child is producing simple two/three word sentences it is suggested that written words, contained in a grammatically correct sentence and displayed on a sentence strip, should be used as a visual prompt, eg. *Please may I have a drink?*

However, there is nothing to suggest you cannot try both. We successfully used the sign for *THE* to help Sam see the word and reinforce it until it became part of his vocabulary.

Playing a game we call *WHERE'S THE..........?* (an early version of 'I Spy') is good fun. Signing and saying the sentence *WHERE'S THE TREE?* for example, encourages turn taking, three word sentences, and can bring a focus to the word *THE*.

Where's the tree?

Research is still in its early days and until recently many people with Down syndrome had very little grammar in their speech. Anything we can do to encourage the development of vocabulary, clarity of speech, the use of grammar and communication skills is a positive step towards independence and inclusion in our society.

So please enjoy learning the signs in this book and using them with your child - it really is fun!

Dr Wendy Uttley

ABOUT THE GRAPHICS

THE IMPORTANCE OF THE FACE IN SIGNING

It is natural for learners to concentrate on the hands and the sign formations when first learning the signs, so try to remember to use your natural body language and facial expressions when you sign.

- **Eye-contact** is important to communication as well as listening.
- Signing can be dull and lose meaning without appropriate **body language** and **facial expression**. Try to use this positively and be expressive.
- Our **face** can convey so much of what we feel and our true meanings, even if we are not conscious of it at the time.

The sign drawings include facial expression where they are appropriate to the main meaning of the signs and to act as a prompt and reminder of the importance of facial expressions.

BSL HANDSHAPES

These are some of the frequently used handshapes in BSL and the terms used in this book to describe them.

Fist

The hand is tightly closed and the thumb is across the fingers.

Clawed Hand

The fingers are extended and bent and spread apart.

Bunched Hand

The finger ends and thumb are bunched together.

Bent Hand

The fingers are straight and together and bent at the palm knuckles.

Closed Hand

The hand is closed and the thumb is against the index finger.

Irish 'T' Hand

(From 'T' in Irish fingerspelling)
The hand is closed with the index finger bent round the top of the thumb.

Flat Hand

The fingers are straight and together.

Open Hand

The fingers and thumb are straight and spread apart.

'L' Hand

The hand is closed with the index finger and thumb extended in an L shape.

'Y' Hand

The hand is closed with the little finger and thumb extended.

'C' Hand

The hand is closed with the index finger and thumb extended and curved in a C shape.

Full 'C' Hand

The thumb is curved and fingers are together and curved in a 'C' shape.

'O' Hand

The tip of the index finger touches the tip of the thumb to form an 'O' shape.

Full 'O' Hand

The tips of fingers and thumb are held together to form an 'O' shape.

'M' Hand

The index, middle and ring fingers are extended, straight and held together.

'N' Hand

The index and middle fingers are extended, together and straight.

'V' Hand

The index and middle fingers are extended and spread apart.

Index

The index finger is extended from a closed hand.

USING FINGERSPELLING

Fingerspelling represents each letter of the alphabet on the hands and can be used to spell out whole words, abbreviated forms or initials and gives a direct link to written English.

- With young children we suggest you fingerspell the initial letter of their name as you say their name, eg. 'S' as you say 'Sam'.

This is very useful since many children with Down syndrome tend to miss off the initial sound of words in their speech, including their own name; Sam was 'am' until he was about five years old. Signing the 'S' as you say 'Sam' brings focus to, and practice of, the initial sound.

Fingerspell the initial letter of all other children and staff in the classroom, eg. Mrs Jones would be fingerspelt as 'J' (you would still say 'Mrs Jones'). This enables the child with Down syndrome to learn their names, thus promoting communication and independence.

- You can fingerspell key syllable letters in a long word to help pronunciation, eg. Trou**S**ers.

- You can use it for abbreviated forms eg **JAN** - JANUARY and repeated initials eg. **KK** - KITCHEN, and so on.

FINGERSPELLING ALPHABETS

Full colour A4 charts for right and left-handed fingerspelling alphabets are available as free downloads from **www.deafbooks.co.uk/downloads**
Downloads also include Winter Weather and Numbers Quick Reference Guide.

CREATING INDIVIDUALISED MATERIALS

The graphics packs referred to on page 6 contain separate folders of line drawings and colour graphics. A comprehensive set in adult characters and a smaller sub-set in children's characters are available in various package options.

| A social worker | will be | on duty | at the centre | on Wednesday | afternoon |

ADULT COLOUR SET

| A social worker | will be | on duty | at the centre | on Wednesday | afternoon |

CHILDREN'S SET BLACK AND WHITE LINE DRAWINGS

| five | little | monkeys | jumping on | the bed |

CHILDREN'S COLOUR SET

| five | little | monkeys | jumping on | the bed |

The graphics can be used to convey BSL sign order or as Sign Supported English (SSE) with written text as above, and also to reinforce BSL vocabulary with pictures and symbols as shown on the right in which the Let's Sign BSL graphics are used with Widgit Symbols.
See www.widgit.com

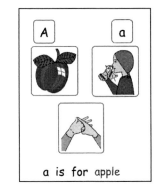

a is for apple

Collaborative work is also underway with Special iApps to trial and develop a range of apps for the Apple iPad.

Please visit www.specialiapps.co.uk for full details.

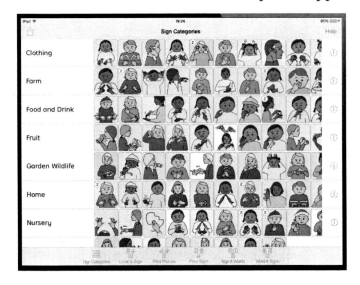

The apps contain sign graphics and variations, matching pictures, written words and optional use of spoken words.

The facility to edit and personalise with your own text, photos and spoken words enables the creation of materials to match the very individual needs of each child.

PLEASE

Tips of flat hand touch mouth, then hand swings forward/down to finish palm up.

THANK YOU, THANKS

Tips of flat hand touch mouth, then hand swings forward/down to finish palm up.

HELLO, HI

Flat hand with thumb tucked in makes short movement out from near side of head.

GOOD

Closed hand with thumb up makes short movement forward. Two hands for **VERY GOOD**.

MORNING

Fingertips of R. bent hand (with thumb up) touch left then right side of chest.

BYE, GOODBYE, CHEERIO

Hand moves side to side in waving movement.

AFTERNOON

Tips of 'N' hand touch chin, then hand twists from wrist to point forwards.

YES

Closed hand nods up and down twice.

NO

Flat hand swings emphatically to the right as the head shakes. Can be both hands starting crossed moving firmly apart.

I

Tip of extended index finger contacts the chest.

ME

Fingertips of 'M' hand contact the chest. This is not a BSL sign.

MINE, MY

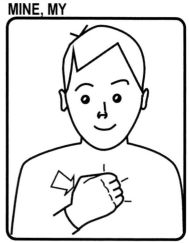

Closed hand moves back to contact chest.

NAME, CALLED

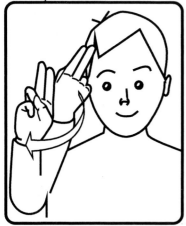

Tips of 'N' hand touch side of forehead, then move and twist forward.

DAD, DADDY, FATHER

Fingers form fingerspelt 'F' and tap twice.

MUM, MUMMY, MOTHER

Repeated fingerspelt 'M'.

FAMILY

Hands form fingerspelt 'F' formation and move round in horizontal circle.

GRANDFATHER, GRANDAD

Fingerspell 'GF'.

GRANDMOTHER, GRANDMA

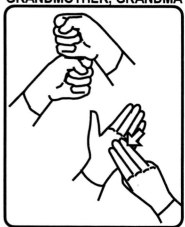

Fingerspell 'GMM', or 'GM' respectively.

BROTHER

Knuckles of closed hands rub up and down against each other.

SISTER

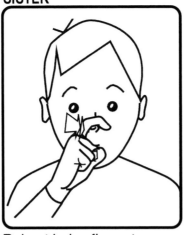

R. bent index finger taps twice on nose.

AUNTIE, UNCLE

Tips of bent 'V' hand tap chin twice.

NANA, NAN

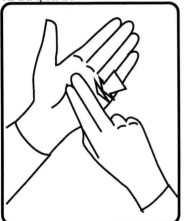

Fingerspell 'N' and tap twice.

MAN

Fingers and thumb stroke down chin and thumb closes onto fingers.

BOY

Extended R. index finger brushes across chin to the left.

CHILDREN

Palm down flat hand moves down, then repeats slightly to the side.

GIRL

Edge of palm forward extended index finger brushes forward twice on cheek.

WOMAN, LADY

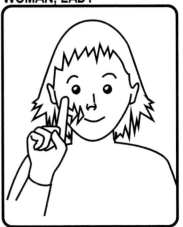

Palm forward index finger brushes forward/down across cheek.

FRIEND

Hands clasp together and shake forward/down several times.

DOCTOR

Tips of R. hand index finger and thumb grasp left wrist.

JESUS

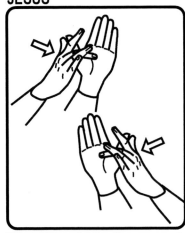

Tip of R. middle finger prods into L. palm, then reverse L. into R.

KING

Tips of clawed hand touch side of head, then fingers and thumb stroke down chin.

QUEEN

Tips of clawed hand touch side of head, then palm forward index finger strokes forward/down on cheek.

POLICE

Fingers of R. 'V' hand flex as hand is drawn across back of L. wrist.

MAGIC, MAGICIAN

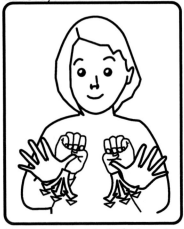

Palm forward full 'O' hands spring forward and open twice.

BABY

Arms move from side to side in rocking movements.
Without movement for **DOLL**.

SANTA, SACK

Fists grip imaginary sack over shoulder with repeated up and down movments.

ANIMAL

Clawed hands make repeated alternate forward circular movements.

PET

R. flat hand strokes back of L. closed hand.

DOG

'N' hands are held like a dog begging, with two short downward movements.

BIRD

Index finger and thumb open and close in front of mouth. Elbows may move in and out (CHICKEN).

RABBIT

Palm forward 'N' hands held at sides of head twitch forwards several times.

CAT

Fingers flex as hands make short repeated outward movements from sides of mouth.

FISH

Flat hand moves diagonally forward with quick wiggling movements from the wrist.

DEER, REINDEER

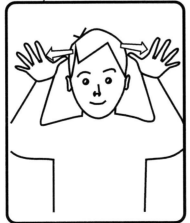

Thumbs of open hands on sides of head; hands move slightly forward and apart.

SHEEP

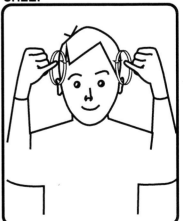

Extended little fingers make forward circles from sides of head.

DUCK

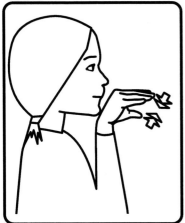

Fingers of bent hand (or 'N' hand) open and close onto thumb several times, in front of chin.

DONKEY

Thumbs of flat hands contact sides of forehead and hands twist from wrists several times.

PIG

Fist moves round in small circles in front of nose.

COW

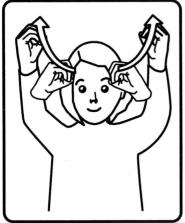

Full 'O' hands move upwards and outwards from the sides of the forehead in shape of horns.

HORSE, PONY, RIDE

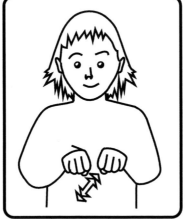

Palm down closed hands make repeated movements forward/down.

HORSE

Fingers of R. 'V' hand are placed astride L. flat hand.

FROG

Fingers of 'V' hand flick out sideways twice under the chin.

FLY

'O' hand moves across in small waggling movements from the wrist.

BUTTERFLY

Hands are crossed with thumbs interlocked, and hands bend from wrists in flapping movements.

BIKE, PEDAL

Closed hands make alternate forward circular motions.

CAR, DRIVE

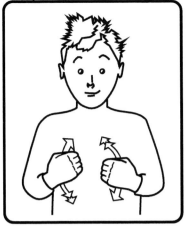

Closed hands move in action of holding and moving a steering wheel.

BUS, LORRY, TRUCK, VAN

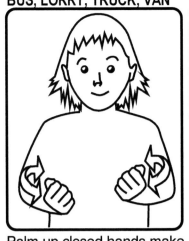

Palm up closed hands make wide flat steering movements.

TRACTOR

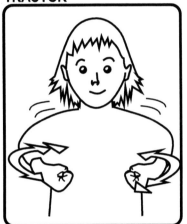

Palm up fists make forward and back steering movements as body and shoulders shake up and down.

AEROPLANE, FLY

Closed hand with thumb and little finger extended moves in action of a plane flying.

POLICE CAR

Fingertips of R. bent 'V' hand are drawn across the back of L. wrist, then fists move in action of steering wheel.

BOAT

Tips of flat hands touch, hands held at an angle move forwards in up and down bobbing movement.

TRAIN, RAILWAY

Closed hand (or fist) makes forward circular motions at side of body, or single firm movement forward.

MOTORBIKE

Both hands in fists are held palms facing down; R. hand twists upwards twice.

EAT, FOOD

Bunched hand makes two
short movements to the
mouth.

HUNGRY

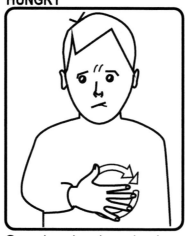

Open hand makes circular
rubbing movements on
stomach.

DINNER

'N' hands move up and down
to the mouth alternately.
Also means **MEAL**.

MILK

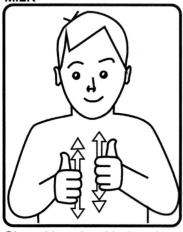

Closed hands with thumbs
up move up and down
alternately.

DRINK

Full 'C' hand moves to mouth
with small backward tipping
movement.

COFFEE

'C' hand makes short quick
twisting movements near
side of mouth.

TEA, CAFE, CUP OF TEA

'O' hand moves up and tips
slightly back to the mouth.

CHOCOLATE

Edge of bent index finger
brushes down chin twice.

SWEET

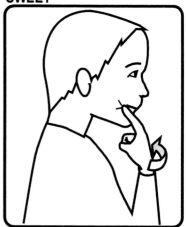

Tip of index finger at side of
mouth twists from palm left to
palm back.

APPLE

Full 'C' hand twists upwards and forwards from the wrist near the mouth like taking a bite.

ORANGE (fruit and colour)

Clawed hand makes repeated squeezing movements near side of mouth. **Colours vary.**

BANANA

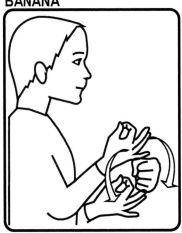

Mime holding and peeling a banana.

GRAPE

L. bunched hand held pointing downwards; tips of R. bunched hand make action of twisting grape from bunch.

PEAR

R. 'N' hand makes soft brushing movements, twisting from palm left to palm back at side of mouth.

TOMATO

R. bunched hand twists against the end of L. index finger, or L. bunched hand.

SAUSAGES

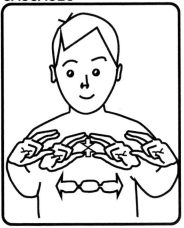

'N' hands open and close onto thumbs several times as hands move apart.

EGG

Palm up R. 'N' hand makes slicing movement across top of L. fist.

CHIPS

Index and thumbs close together repeatedly in small outward movements indicating the outline shape.

ICE-CREAM, CORNET

Fist makes repeated downward brushing movements near mouth, tongue slightly out.

YOGHURT

Fingerspell 'Y' then fingers of R. 'N' hand dip into L. 'O' hand and move to mouth as if eating from a pot.

BISCUIT

Tips of R. clawed hand tap twice against left elbow.

BREAD

Edge of R. flat hand moves in slicing action across L. palm.

CHEESE

Fingertips of R. bent hand rest on L. palm as R. hand twists repeatedly from the wrist.

CAKE, BUN, SCONE

Tips of R. clawed hand tap twice on back of L. hand. Also means **ROLL, SMALL PIE.**

MASH, MASHED POTATO

R. fist stamps up and down on L. palm several times.

POTATO

R. thumb moves over palm up L. full 'C' hand in action of holding and peeling a potato.

VEGETABLE, VEGETARIAN

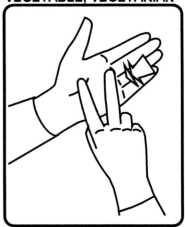

Hands form fingerspelt 'V' with repeated movement.

CARROT

Fist held at side of mouth makes sharp twisting movement as if holding and taking a bite from a carrot.

SANDWICH

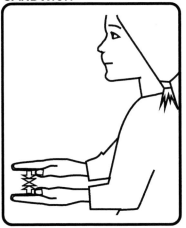

Flat hands pat together twice, palm to palm.

HOT

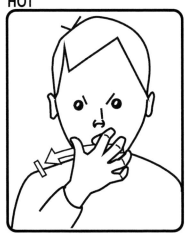

Clawed hand is drawn sharply across the mouth. Can be flat hand drawn across forehead then shaken.

CRISPS

R. 'O' hand moves repeatedly up to mouth from L. palm. Bunched hand may be used.

BAKED BEANS

Hands form repeated fingerspelt 'BB'.

FRUIT

Fingers waggle as R. hand moves from right to left under the chin.

JUICE

Fingers of palm back open hand wiggle as hand moves downwards from the chin.

CHEW, CHEW UP

R. closed hand rests on top of L. and moves in anticlockwise circles. The mouth makes chewing movements.

PIZZA

Fingerspelt 'P' 'Z' followed by R. index pointing down above L. palm moves round in circle.

HOUSE, HOME

Flat hands held at an angle, touch at fingertips.

WINDOW

R. palm back flat hand moves up and down on top of L.

TV

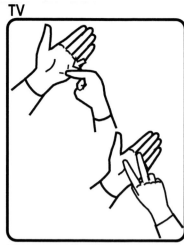

Fingerspell 'TV'.

CHAIR, SEAT

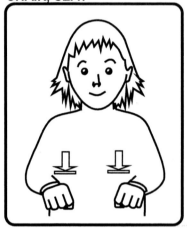

Palm down fists make short firm movement down.

TELEPHONE

'Y' hand held near ear.

BED, SLEEP

Head tilts onto both hands held together. Eyes are closed for **SLEEP**.

DRESS, FROCK, WEAR

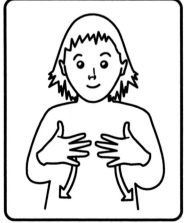

Open hands brush down chest and apart finishing palm down.

GET DRESSED

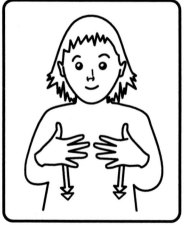

Open hands brush downwards twice on body.

BATH

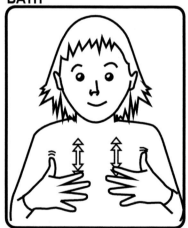

Open hands move up and down chest several times. Closed hands can be used.

COOK

Irish 'T' hand makes whisking movements in crook of left arm.

COOK, PAN

Hand in Irish 'T' handshape makes repeated shaking movements forward/back.

SPOON, SOUP

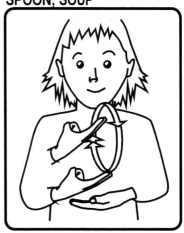

Palm up 'N' hand makes repeated upward circular movements to the mouth from L. palm.

KNIFE, CUTLERY

Middle finger edge of R. 'N' hand makes small sawing movements on L. 'N' hand. Also means RESTAURANT.

FORK

Tips of index and middle finger prod into L. palm.

PLATE

R. index finger pointing down makes small circles around L. palm.

TOWEL

Closed hands move in action of holding and drying with a bath towel.

CD-ROM

Knuckles of R. 'Y' hand contact L. palm as R. hand twists repeatedly from the wrist.

DOOR, GATE

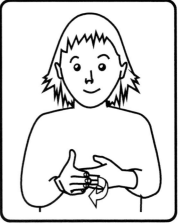

R. hand pivots forwards and back from wrist in front of L.

TOOTHBRUSH

Irish 'T' hand (or index finger) makes brushing movements near the mouth.   Also means **CLEAN (DO) ONE'S TEETH.**

COMB, COMB YOUR HAIR

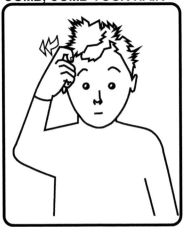

Irish 'T' hand moves in action of using a hair comb.

BRUSH (hair)

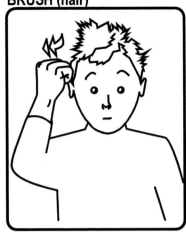

Closed hand moves in action of brushing hair near side of head.

NAPPY

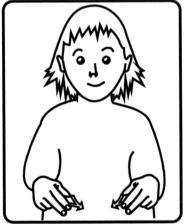

Fingers of 'N' hands snap shut onto thumbs at sides of lower body.

KISS

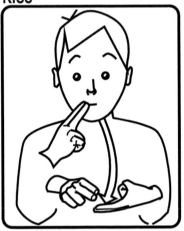

Tips of R. 'N' hand contact lips, then move down to contact tips of L. 'N' hand.

TOY/S

Hands in fingerspelt 'T' formation move in small circular movements.

TOILET, TOILETS

Tip of middle finger rubs up and down on left side of chest.

WEE WEE

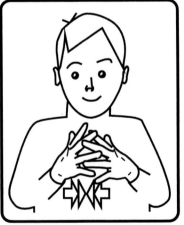

Fingers form fingerspelt 'W' with two movements.

POTTY

R. index finger pointing down moves in circle above and to the right of L. fist.

LAUGH, FUN, FUNNY

'C' hand makes small shaking movements under the chin.

CROSS, ANGRY

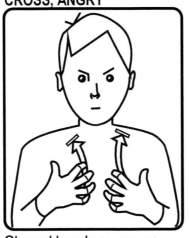

Clawed hands move up body sharply twisting to palm up, cheeks puffed, brows furrowed.

SAD

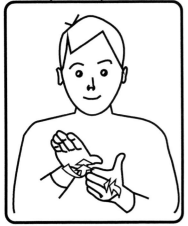

Palm left R. flat hand moves down in front of nose. Mouth and shoulders droop.

HAPPY, ENJOY, GLAD

Hands make repeated contact brushing against each other, with pleased expression.

LOVE, DEAR

Flat hands (or closed hands) are held crossed on the chest.

WARM

Clawed hand makes small circling movements in front of mouth.

COLD

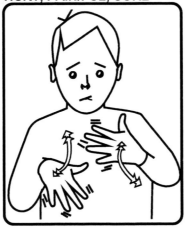

Closed hands and elbows pull into body in shivering action, shoulders hunched, cheeks puffed.

HURT, PAIN/FUL, SORE

Palm back open hands shake alternately up and down from the wrists with pained expression.

FRIGHTENED, SCARED

Tips of clawed hands tap chest twice as body cringes backwards.

CRY, TEARS

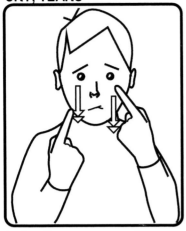

Index fingers move down cheeks under eyes alternately. One hand may be used.

SORRY

Closed hand rubs in circular movements on the chest with sorrowful expression.

ILL, POORLY, NOT WELL

Little fingers (or just one hand) brush down the chest. The head may tilt and movement repeat. Also means **TIRED**.

SICK, THROW UP, VOMIT

Open hand brushes upwards on chest, and up past the mouth tipping forward to palm up.

HOSPITAL, AMBULANCE

R. thumb tip draws cross on left upper arm. Also one version of **NURSE**.

MEDICINE

Extended R. little finger makes circular movements inside L. cupped hand.

GLASSES, SPECTACLES

Index fingers circle the eyes in outline of glasses.

BETTER

Tip of R. extended thumb makes two small forward brushing movements against top of L. thumb.

WORSE

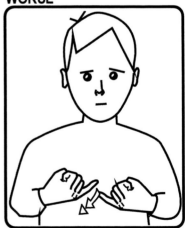

R. little finger brushes downwards twice off L. little finger. Brows are furrowed.

SCHOOL

Palm back flat hand makes side to side or circular movements in front of mouth.

NURSERY

Tip of extended middle finger brushes down chin twice.

TEACH/ER

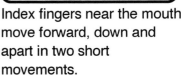

Index fingers near the mouth move forward, down and apart in two short movements.

ASSEMBLY

Open hands held apart and facing, twist over and down towards each other. Fingers indicate a gathering of people.

BOOK, READ

Flat hands start palm to palm, then twist open and apart. Wiggle slightly from side to side for **READ.**

PEN, PENCIL

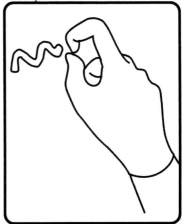

Bent index and thumb tip in contact; hand moves to the right in small squiggles, or across L. palm.

MUSIC

Extended index fingers swing in and out towards each other several times.

PAPER

Tap knuckles of both closed hands together twice.

BALL, FOOTBALL

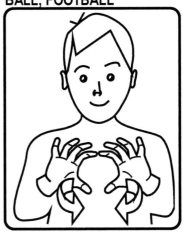

Hands with fingers curved move round and apart in shape of large ball.

CORRIDOR, HALL

'N' hands move forward at sides of head. Flat hands can be used.

TABLE

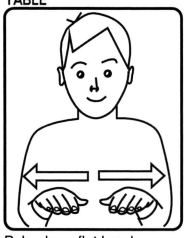

Palm down flat hands move apart.

SIGN

Hands circle forward round each other several times.

WORK

Edge of R. flat hands makes short forward tapping movements on L. at right angles.

CLEVER

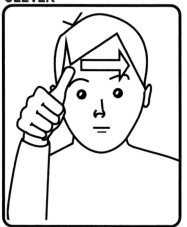

Tip of extended thumb moves sharply right to left across the forehead.

DIFFICULT, HARD

Tip of R. thumb prods into L. palm twice.

UNIFORM, SMART

Tips of extended thumbs move simultaneously down the chest.

SAND, SOIL

Thumbs rub across pads of fingers in crumbling action as hands move upwards. Also means **FLOUR**.

COMPUTER

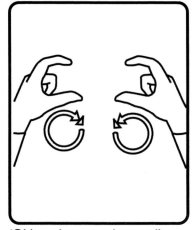

'C' hands move in small simultaneous circular movements.

WATER

Palm down open hand moves sideways in wavy up and down motion.

COAT, JACKET

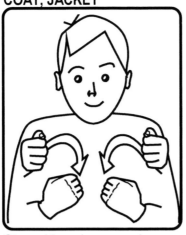

Closed hands move down and round from shoulders in action of putting coat on.

BAG, SHOPPING

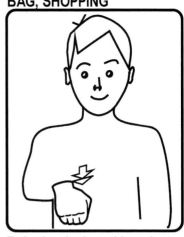

Palm back closed hand makes short repeated downward movements.

TEDDY, CUDDLE

Closed hands are crossed and tap twice, hugging into chest.

SING, SONG, CAROL

Palm back 'V' hand makes spiralling upward movements from near mouth.

PLAY, GAME

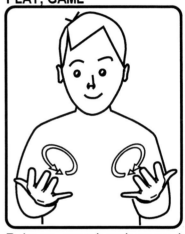

Palm up open hands move in simultaneous circular movements.

SCISSORS, CUT

Fingers of 'V' hand open and close twice.

WASH, WASH HANDS

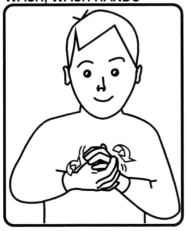

Hands rub together, or rub on appropriate part of body. Also means **SOAP**.

CLASS, CLASSROOM

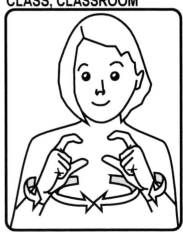

'C' hands face each other then twist apart and round to finish touching with palms facing back.

BREAK

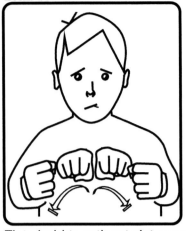

Fists held together twist apart in snapping action.

SIT DOWN

Palm down flat hands, one on top of the other, make short firm movement down.

HURRY, BE QUICK

R. index finger taps quickly up and down on L. index finger several times.

WALK

Fingers of 'V' hand wiggle as hand moves forward or in *direction* to suit context.

GET UP, STAND UP

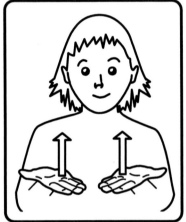

Palm up flat hands move upwards.

SAY, TELL

Index moves forward from the mouth. Used for **TALK** and similar meanings.

MORE

R. flat hand taps down on top of L. fist.

STOP, WAIT, HOLD ON

Palm forward flat hand makes a short firm forward movement. Repeats for **WAIT**, **HOLD ON** etc.

FINISH

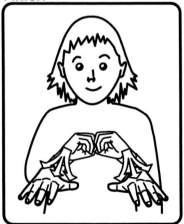

'O' hands contact each other, then hands spring open, down and apart.

HELP

Closed hand with thumb up rests on L. palm as hands move forward together.

COME, COME BACK

Index finger held forward moves back to body. Index finger may be bent or flex (**COME HERE**).

GO, GONE, WENT, SENT

Index finger swings forward/up from wrist to point forward.

SEE, LOOK

Index finger moves forward from eye. Can also be signed with 'V' hand.

LISTEN, HEAR

Cupped hand held behind ear.

AGAIN, REPEAT

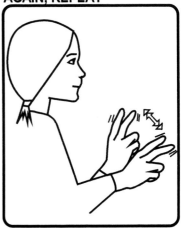

Palm left 'V' hand makes short quick shaking movements forward/down from the wrist.

JUMP

R. 'V' hand jumps up flexing on L. palm or in way to suit context. Repeated for **BABY BOUNCER, TRAMPOLINE.**

SLOW, SLOWLY

R. index finger brushes from left wrist up the forearm. Also means **LONG TIME.**

STAND

R. 'V' hand stands on L. palm.

COLOUR

Palm forward open hand makes anticlockwise circular movements.

BLUE

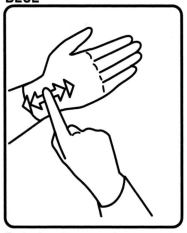

R. index finger rubs to and fro on L. wrist, or on back of L. hand.

GREEN

R. flat hand sweeps up left forearm.

PINK

Palm left R. index moves down in front of nose.

BROWN

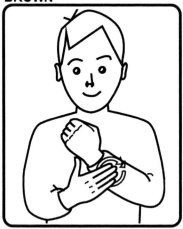

R. hand rubs in small circles on left forearm.

YELLOW

Fingerspell 'Y' and make small repeated brushing movements with R. index.

WHITE

Tips of 'O' hand make small repeated brushing movements near the collar.

PURPLE

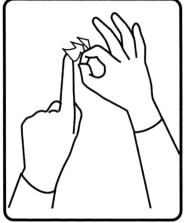

Form fingerspelt 'P' and make small forward brushing movements off L. index with R 'O' hand.

RED

R. index finger brushes to the left across the bottom lip.

BLACK

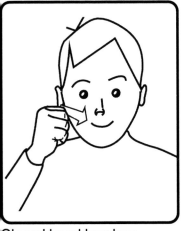

Closed hand brushes forward/down on side of cheek.

GOLD, GOLDEN

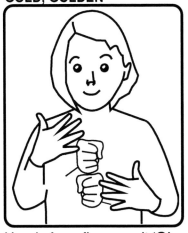

Hands form fingerspelt 'G' then spring open and apart.

SILVER

Hands form fingerspelt 'S', then hands spring open and apart.

RAINBOW

Palm forward full 'C' hand moves over in large arc.

ORANGE (fruit and colour)

Clawed hand makes repeated squeezing movements near side of mouth.

SAME, LIKE, TOO

Index fingers pointing forward contact each other. May tap twice or make single contact.

DIFFERENT

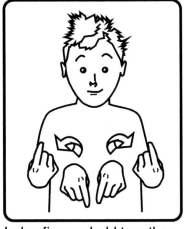

Index fingers held together twist over and apart.

CLEAN

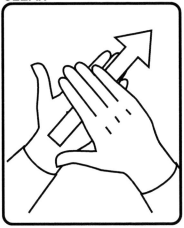

R. hand brushes forward/right along L. palm.

DIRTY, GRIMY, MUCKY

Closed hands rub together at the wrists with appropriate facial expression.

BIG

Open hands move apart in small arcs with emphasis.

SMALL, LITTLE

Palm facing hands make two short movements towards each other, shoulders slightly hunched.

LITTLE, BIT, TINY

Index and thumb indicate small amount.

HEAVY

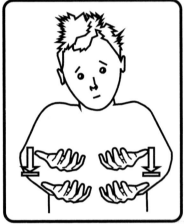

Palm up hands move down with stress (may repeat) shoulders sag.

BEAUTIFUL

Tips of bunched hand spring forward and open from the lips.

OLD

Fingers of 'V' hand flex as hand moves down in front of nose.

NEW

R. flat hand brushes sharply up behind L.

DRY

Thumbs rub across the fingertips from little fingers to indexes. One hand can be used.

WET

Fingers of bent hand open and close onto thumb several times. Two hands can be used.

UNDER

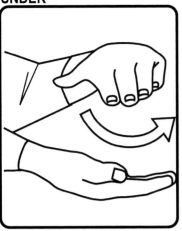

Palm up R. hand moves forward under palm down L hand in small arc.

IN

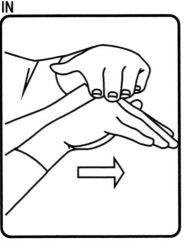

R. bent hand straightens to a flat hand as it moves forward under L. hand.

ON (physically), PUT ON

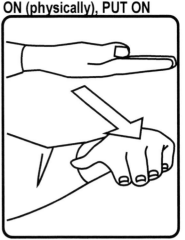

Back of R. flat hand is placed on back of L.

OVER

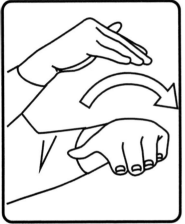

R. bent hand moves over L. hand in small arc.

UP

Index finger points up and makes small upward movement. Repeated movement for UPSTAIRS.

DOWN

Index finger points down and makes small downward movement. Also means THIS, HERE, DOWNSTAIRS (may repeat).

BETWEEN, IN BETWEEN

R. flat hand slots between the middle and ring fingers of L. hand and waggles from side to side.

NEXT TO, BESIDE

Closed hands with thumbs extended; R. hand twists from the wrist to the right, away from L. (R. hand only for NEXT, TURN).

NICE

R. thumb moves across chin from left to right.

SUN, SUNNY

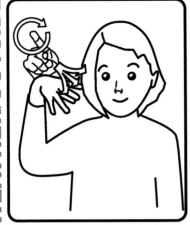

Index finger makes circle at head height, then changes to full hand opening with downward movement.

WIND, WINDY

Palm back open hands waft back to face several times.

SNOW, SNOWING

Fingers wiggle as hands move down in small wavy movements.

RAIN, DRIZZLE

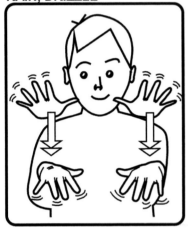

Open hands make two movements down, the fingers may wiggle slightly, or may move with force.

COLD, WINTER

Closed hands and elbows pull into body in shivering action, shoulders hunched.

FOG, FOGGY

Palm forward open hands move down and cross over in front of face, eyes slightly squinted.

ICE, ICY

Palm down open hands held out in front of body, move back flexing to clawed hands. Also means **FREEZE, FREEZING, FROZEN.**

SUMMER, HOT WEATHER

Flat hand strokes left to right across forehead.

CLOUD, CLOUDY

Palm forward clawed hands make repeated alternate circling movements.

40

LIGHTNING

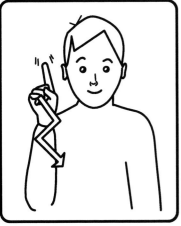

Palm forward index moves downward sharply in zigzag.

OUTSIDE

Bent hand makes two short forward movements.

SEA, OCEAN, WATER

Palm down open hand moves sideways in wavy up and down motion. Can be both hands.

SKY, HEAVENS

Bent hands move apart in small arc over the head.

STARS

Middle finger tips flick out from thumbs as hands move out in small arcs at head height.

FARM/ER

Closed hand, thumb out moves from chest in forward arc to re-contact body. For **FARM**, add sideways sweep of palm down flat hand.

TREE

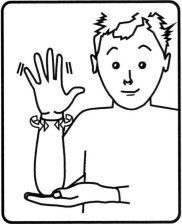

R. open hand upright and resting on L. hand, twists repeatedly from the wrist.

FLOWER

'O' (or bunched) hand moves from side to side under nose, like sniffing a flower. For **GARDEN**, add sweep of palm down flat hand.

GRASS

Fingers of R. hand wiggle as they move along behind left forearm.

DAY, LIGHT

Palm back open hands start crossed and swing upwards and apart.

EVENING, NIGHT, TONIGHT

Palm back flat hands swing in/down to finish crossed.

MORNING

Fingertips of R. bent hand (with thumb up) touch left then right side of chest.

AFTERNOON

Tips of 'N' hand touch chin, then hand twists from wrist to point forwards.

YESTERDAY

Index finger on side of cheek twists back/down onto shoulder.

TOMORROW

Index finger on side of cheek twists forward/down from the wrist to finish palm up.

NOW

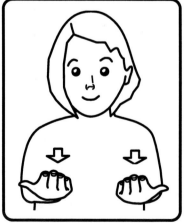

Palm up flat hands make single firm movement down.

TODAY

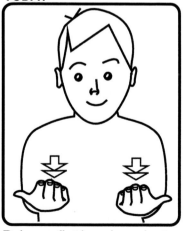

Palm up flat hands make two short movements down.

WEEK, ONE WEEK

Extended index finger moves forward along left forearm. Two fingers extended for **TWO WEEKS** and so on.

SUNDAY

Flat hands tap together twice. **Varies**. Without movement also means **PRAY/ER.**

MONDAY

Fingerpelt initial 'M'. Followed by sign for 'DAY' (not in BSL).

TUESDAY

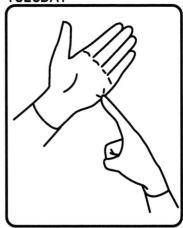

Fingerpelt initial 'T'. Followed by sign for 'DAY' (not in BSL).

WEDNESDAY

Fingerpelt initial 'W'. Followed by sign for 'DAY' (not in BSL).

THURSDAY

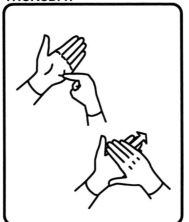

Fingerpell 'TH'. Followed by sign for 'DAY' (not in BSL).

FRIDAY

Fingerpelt initial 'F'. Followed by sign for 'DAY' (not in BSL).

SATURDAY

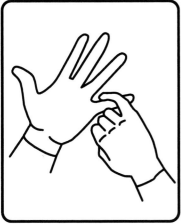

Fingerpelt initial 'S'. Followed by sign for 'DAY' (not in BSL).

BIRTHDAY

Flat hands near sides of waist move forward/in and then upwards and apart.

CHRISTMAS

R. hand brushes down across back of L. then closes and contacts back of L. hand again.

WHY?

Edge of R. index taps side of left upper chest twice, eyebrows raised or furrowed.

BECAUSE

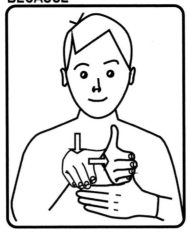

R. flat hand contacts index edge of L. hand, then twists and moves left to touch inside of L. thumb.

WHICH?

'Y' hand moves from side to side or between the objects or persons referred to, eyebrows raised or furrowed.

WHEN?

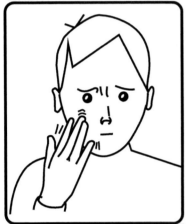

Fingers wiggle at side of face, eyebrows raised or furrowed.

WHO?

Index finger makes small horizontal circles, eyebrows raised or furrowed.

WANT, NEED

Flat hand brushes down side of chest twisting to palm down.

WHERE?

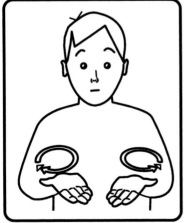

Palm up hands move in small outward circles, or hands may move in-out towards each other, eyebrows raised or furrowed.

WHAT? WHAT FOR?

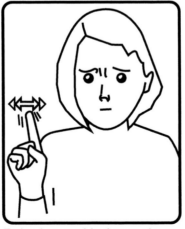

Palm forward index makes small side to side shaking movements, eyebrows raised or furrowed.

HOW MANY

Knuckles of closed hand tap chin twice. With raised eyebrows can also mean **NUMBER, DATE, MATHS.**

HOW OLD? WHAT AGE?

Fingers wiggle in front of nose. Eyebrows are raised or furrowed.

HOW MUCH

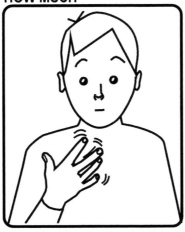

Hand held palm back with fingers wiggling. Eyebrows are raised or furrowed.

TIME, WHAT TIME?

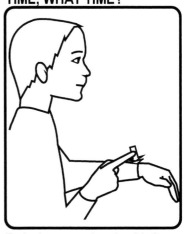

R. index taps back of left wrist twice. With brows raised or furrowed means **WHAT TIME?**

HOW ARE YOU?

Closed hands with thumbs up twist shaply over from palm down to palms facing.

AND, IN ADDITION

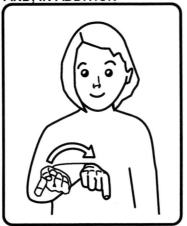

Extended index finger flips over and inwards from palm up to palm down. This is not a BSL sign.

THE

Palm forward 'O' hand moves to the right.   This is not a BSL sign.

YOU

Index points with short movement towards referent (with eye gaze).

YOUR, YOURS

Palm forward closed hand is directed towards referent (with eye gaze).

HERE, THIS

Index finger makes two short downward movements. Two hands can be used. Also means **DOWNSTAIRS.**

SOME SENTENCES TO PRACTISE SIGNING

Try practising some of these in a role play session. Take turns to be the child and think about how you would go about communicating your needs and also how you would respond as an adult. Remember you need to be modelling the signed and the spoken word in your response.

Try also to think about what words and signs you are using to communicate, for example the phrase '*do you want to play in the sand?*' could be reworded so that it doesn't just require a *yes* or *no* answer. '*Do you want to play in the sand or water?*' is better, since it gives a choice and thus provides an opportunity for the child to practise language. Then you need to think about what signs you will use - you will probably only sign *PLAY SAND* and *PLAY WATER* but you will say the full sentence.

SHORT PHRASES YOU MIGHT LIKE TO PRACTISE SIGNING AND SAYING

Good Listening
Please get dressed
Stand up
Stop
Please
Thank you
Please sit here
Look at the teacher
Good sitting
Listen to the teacher
Listen
Sit here

Good afternoon
Good morning
Where's your book
Where are your shoes
Good work
Good reading
Look at me
Look at this
Look here
Good eating
Sit down

LONGER SENTENCES - SIGN KEY WORDS

Which one do you want?
Which ones are the same?
Who do you want to sit with?
Please put your things away.
Come here now.
Sit down on your chair now.
Please walk slowly.
Come here quickly.
What do you want to do? This or that?

What do you want to eat?
Why did this happen?
Who do you want to play with?
Please eat up your dinner.
Chew up your food/crisps/sandwiches.
Get undressed for your bath please.
Hello, how are you today?
Do you want chips or mashed potato?

AMBULANCE

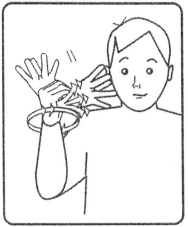

Full 'O hand opens and closes repeatedly as it swivels from wrist near side of head.

BIRTHDAY

Edge of R. 'O' hand taps upper left chest twice.

BROWN

L. fist held upwards; knuckles of R. fist rub in circles on left arm.

CARPET TIME

Palm down flat hand sweeps sideways then R. index taps back of L. wrist twice.

CARPET TIME, SIT DOWN

One hand on top of the other as both hands make downward movement.

COMB

Clawed hand makes combing movements on side of head.

DIWALI

R. middle finger flicks repeatedly off thumb as hand rests on back of palm down L. hand

DON'T LIKE

Open hand on chest twists over and away from the body as the head shakes with negative expression.

DRAW

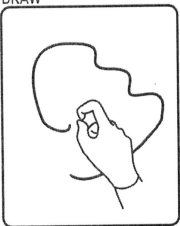

Hand holds imaginary pencil and moves round in wavy movements.

DVD

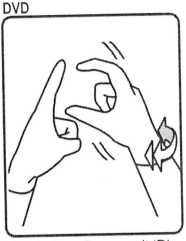

Hands form fingerspelt 'D' formation as R. hand twists repeatedly at the wrist.

EID

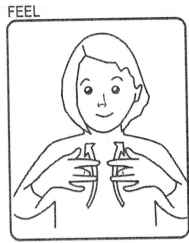

Index and middle finger open and close in crescent shape above the head then middle finger flicks off thumb several times.

FEEL

Middle fingers brush upwards on the body.

FIRE ENGINE

Both hands facing move alternately up and down with fingers flickering then fists move in steering wheel action.

GATE

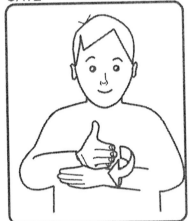

Left hand held across front of body, both hands palm back; right arm swings forward from elbow away from the left.

GIRL

Palm left index finger makes two small brushing movements near side of the mouth.

GOD

Index finger twists sharply up/back from the wrist near the side of the head.

HIDE

Flat hands move side to side across each other in front of the face.

HOSPITAL, NURSE

R. thumb tip (or index tip) draws a cross on left upper arm.

IPAD

Tip of R. middle finger swipes across the L. palm several times.

LIKE

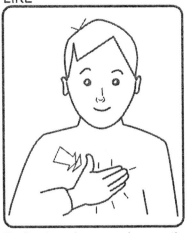

R. flat hand taps twice on the chest.

MOHAMMED

Fingerspell 'P' 'M' then fingers and thumb brush down chin as thumb closes onto fingers.

MONTH

Fingerspell 'M'.

NURSE

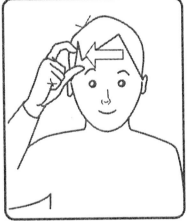

Tips of 'C' hand are drawn across the forehead.

PICTURE

Index fingers move out, down and back together in outline shape.

PRINCE

Edge of palm up flat hand moves diagonally down the body from the left shoulder.

PRINCESS

Index fingers and thumb on head move out/down as they close together in tiara outline shape.

RAMADAN

Fingerspell 'R' then open hand rubs in circles on the abdomen.

SHARE

R. flat hand on L. palm waggles side to side as both hands move backwards and forwards.

SHOE

Palm down R. full 'C' hand (or palm up) slots onto L. hand. Repeat L. onto R. for plural.

SOCKS

'O' hands make short upward pulling movement near right, then left side of body.

TOAST

Palm facing flat hands make short abrupt upward movement like toast popping up.

TOGETHER

Fingers of L. 'N' hand hold fingers of R. 'N' hand.

SENTENCES A CHILD MIGHT TRY TO COMMUNICATE

I like bananas.
I don't want carrots.
I'm hungry.
I like my teacher.
It is windy today.
I want some paper.
I like school.
My head is hurting.
I want to play outside.
Please play that music again.
I want to draw a picture.
I have broken my pencil.
Can I have a drink of
water/milk?
My hands are dirty.

I want my dinner.
I want to go home.
I want you to do that again.
I am tired.
Help me.
I'm finished.
I want a turn.
Please may I have a biscuit?
I want my mummy.
My daddy is at work.
My brother is at home.
I want an apple.
My sister's name is Anne.
I don't like that it scares me.

I like bananas.

Please may I have a biscuit?

Today is windy.

My daddy is at work.

I want some paper.

Help me.

Please play that music again.

I'm tired.

47

EARLY LANGUAGE DEVELOPMENT ACTIVITIES

These activities are helpful in encouraging early communication skills.

- Try to avoid any distractions - turn off the TV and radio.
- Try to be as animated as possible and give lots of praise for any success.
- Continue for only as long as the child is interested.

Teach the signs to your child by demonstrating and by guiding their hands if needed. Children with Down syndrome usually pick up signs quite quickly.

Don't worry if the child signs the word in their own way - for example, pats top of arm rather than elbow for *BISCUIT* - it's the communication that is important.

You in turn will sign the sign correctly and say the spoken word loud and clear, firstly in isolation and then in a sentence eg. *BISCUIT?* Do you want a *BISCUIT* to *EAT?*

LIKE	**TOGETHER/WITH**	**SHARE**
		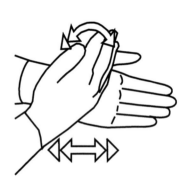
Flat hand taps on chest.	R. hand fingers grasp L.	Hands waggle to and fro, R. edge rests on L.

Sign key words and give lots of encouragement, eg. *Do you LIKE that? - let's do it TOGETHER - shall we SHARE it?*

Remember to always say the words as you sign. Talk to your child and/or sing to them all the time - its easy to forget to do this when a child is not talking - don't let this stop you!

ROLL THE BALL - sit on the floor with a medium sized ball, facing your child. Say and sign the child's name (first letter), let's call the child *SAM,* signed 'S', wait until he makes eye contact and then roll the ball to him.

Encourage the child to roll the ball back - say and sign *BALL PLEASE* - be as animated as possible - sign and say *THANK YOU* and *WELL DONE!* when the ball is returned.

A sibling or partner could be employed to demonstrate the object of the game and to make it more fun! Encourage the child to say/sign *PLEASE* or *BALL PLEASE* before you to return the ball to him/her.

WELL DONE!

TURN

POST THE BALL - make a hole in the bottom of a shoebox or similar and turn it upside down. Take a small ball, attract the child's attention *LOOK SAM!* and post the ball through the hole. Say/sign *WHERE'S the BALL?* Lift the box and act surprised saying *HERE it is!*

Now its Sam's turn - say *WHO'S NEXT?* and *SAM'S TURN,* signing 'S' and encourage him to take the ball and post it; guide his hand if necessary.

Say/sign *WHERE'S the BALL?* and help find it if necessary - *HERE it is!* Say/sign *MUMMY'S (or DADDY'S!) TURN NOW* and repeat the activity.

BLOW BUBBLES - this is great fun. Initially this activity can be used along the lines of the ball activity above, waiting until the child responds to their name before you blow the bubbles. Blow the bubbles so that the child has to move their head to follow them.

As the child develops the aim is for them to blow their own bubbles.

This activity helps the child to become more aware of their mouth and gain muscle control. Similarly blow through straws or blow feathers - don't worry if your child can't do it at first - its good fun!

BLOW BUBBLES

READ

READ BOOKS with your child. Books with 1 - 4 words on each page are ideal.

Choose familiar repetitive stories. You can make your own books using photos of family and friends and the child's own toys if you wish.

Sign key words as you read.

SNACK TIME offers a wonderful opportunity to stimulate communication development.

MORE

Sit your child to the table and offer them a drink - you can simply say and sign *DRINK?* Guide the child's hand in the *DRINK* sign and then give them the cup. Progress to *DRINK PLEASE* and *THANK YOU* - similarly with crisps, fruit, cereal, or biscuits etc. depending on what your child enjoys.

Give small amounts at a time so they have to keep asking - it is easier to encourage them to ask for something that they really want!

Introduce the concept and sign of *MORE* - this is a simple but very useful word.

HIDE

To encourage **LISTENING SKILLS** it is useful (and fun) to hide a favourite toy which makes a sound - music box etc. beneath a cloth next to you. Show the child what you are doing at first - leave a bit showing or help the child to find it. Say and sign *WHERE IS IT?*

Once the child gets the idea you can hide the toy when the child isn't looking and progress to hiding it behind furniture or in another room etc.

IN THE KITCHEN - take your child into the kitchen with you while you are preparing food or washing or emptying the washing machine and so on. Talk (or sing!) about what you are doing - name items - vegetables or clothing etc. Give them an object to play with such as a potato to roll, a sock or a spoon. Talk about the item.

KITCHEN

There are lots of opportunities for conversation when playing with **SMALL WORLD** i.e. doll's house, farmyard etc.

Talk about what the dolls are doing - eating, going to bed etc. - Say and sign the names of animals and the noises that they make - a good cue to sing 'Old McDonald'! Children seem to be able to focus on small world better than the real world at times.

Old McDonald

SING lots of action songs and songs with signs. Add signs to nursery rhymes - don't worry if the existing gestures to some songs are not signs, eg. Incy Wincy Spider, the gestures are still making the song visual and helping the child to join in. See some of the signing sources in Recommended Resources for some good ideas, and also check out the interactive ebooks from the Let's Sign series.

Some other suggested songs are;

Wind a bobbin up
Incy wincy spider
Humpty Dumpty
Mum and dad and uncle John
The wheels on the bus
Row, row, row your boat
Round and round the garden like a teddy bear
This little piggy
* Criss cross apple sauce

* Words overleaf

And later:

Five little ducks went swimming one day
Five currant buns in a bakers shop
Five little speckled frogs
Five fat sausages sizzling in a pan
Miss Polly had a dolly

Start by singing with your child on your knee helping them to sign it. Then sit them opposite you and let then watch you. If you have a large mirror do it in front of a mirror.

SING

SING as well as talk to your child as much as possible. We have found singing can be a great help when dressing/undressing/doing something they don't particularly want to do/are uncertain about. If you sing anything that comes into your head eg. 'this is the way we put on your sock' (to the tune of *Here we go round the mulberry bush*) it seems to work and it also helps to stop you from getting stressed out with it all!

* Criss Cross Apple Sauce - for babies on knees.

Sit your child on your knee with their back towards you and;

As you say **Criss Cross** - draw a cross on their back with your pointing finger.

As you say **Apple Sauce** - rub round and round on their back with the flat of your hand.

As you say **spider crawling up your back** - scurry your fingers up their back.

As you say **spiders here** - tickle under their left arm.

As you say **spiders there** - tickle under their right arm.

As you say **in your hair** - tickle in their hair.

As you say **a cool breeze** - blow on the back of their neck.

As you say **a tight squeeze** - wrap your arms around them and squeeze them.

As you say **and we all shiver, we all shiver** - jiggle them from side to side, up and down.

Action songs like these are a wonderful opportunity for a *CUDDLE*, a *LAUGH* and why not finish it all off with a *DANCE!*

RECOMMENDED RESOURCES

Down Syndrome Issues & Information (DSii) Booklets:

DSii Speech and Language development for infants with Down syndrome - an overview.

DSii Speech and Language development for infants with Down syndrome-age 0-5.

DSii Speech and Language development for children with Down syndrome-age 5-11.

Down Syndrome Resources and Activities (DSra) Booklets:

DSra Vocabulary checklists and record sheets: Checklist 1- First 120 words.

DSra Vocabulary checklists and record sheets: Checklist 2- Second 340 words.

DSra Vocabulary checklists and record sheets: Checklist 3- Third 350 words.

DSra Speech sounds checklists and record sheets.

DSra Interactive communication and play checklists and record sheets.

DSra Sentences and grammar checklists and record sheets.

Written and produced by the Down Syndrome Educational Trust - details in Useful Contacts overleaf.

Recommended DVDs:

DVD What did you say? A Guide to speech intelligibility in people with Down syndrome. Libby Kumin.

DVD Discovery: Pathways to better speech for children with Down syndrome. Will Shermerhorn.

DVD Inclusion in practise: Educating children with Down syndrome in primary school. Produced by DownsEd.

There are a range of useful nursery rhyme videos and DVDs from Makaton and CBeebies - see website details overleaf.

The Let's Sign Series

DEAFSIGN's developing range of British Sign Language materials, as detailed on page 58

USEFUL CONTACTS

DeafBooks

For the Let's Sign Series
Stockton-on-Tees
TS18 5HH
Tel: 01642 580505
e: cath@deafsign.com
e: info@deafbooks.co.uk
web: www.DeafBooks.co.uk

Down Syndrome Educational International

Leading charity focused on the education and development of individuals with Down syndrome
6 Underley Business Centre
Kirkby Lonsdale
Cumbria
LA6 2DY
Tel: 0300 330 0750 FREE
Fax: 0300 330 0754 FREE
e: info@dseinternational.org
web: www.dseinternational.org

Down's Syndrome Association

National Charity
Langdon Down Centre,
2a Langdon Park,
Teddington,
Middlesex
TW11 9PS
Tel: 0333 1212 300 FREE
e: info@downs-syndrome.org.uk
web: www.downs-syndrome.org.uk

Special iApps

Educational apps for children who are deaf and those with learning disabilities such as autism and Down syndrome
Tel: 0191 375 7903
e: support@specialiapps.co.uk
web: www.specialiapps.co.uk

Symbols Worldwide Ltd T/A Widgit Software

26 Queen Street,
Cubbington,
Leamington Spa
CV32 7NA
Tel: 01926 333680
Fax: 01926 885293
e: info@widgit.com
web: www.widgit.com

The National Deaf Children's Society   (NDCS)

Ground Floor South,
Castle House,
37-45 Paul Street
London
EC2A 4LS
FREEPHONE HELPLINE: 0808 800 8880
Tel: 020 7490 8656
Fax: 020 7251 5020
e: ndcs@ndcs.org.uk
web: www.ndcs.org.uk

USEFUL WEBSITES

www.bbc.co.uk/cbeebies
www.talkfirst.net
www.sign4learning.co.uk
www.familysignlanguage.org.uk
www.nurseryrhymes4u.com

www.signpostbsl.com
www.britishsignlanguage.com
www.mybslbooks.com
www.signedstories.com
www.signbsl.com

INDEX

LET'S SIGN

British Sign Language (BSL)
educational materials from DEAFBOOKS, for
all ages and abilities - Early Years to Adult learners.

Curriculum Support

Dictionaries and Guides

Reward Stickers and Certificates

Songs & Nursery Rhymes

Posters & Flashcards

Interactive ebooks

Low Cost and FREE DOWNLOADS to try
www.DeafBooks.co.uk
Tel: 01642 580505 cath@deafsign.com